The House of a Mouse

The House of a Mouse

Poems by
AILEEN FISHER

illustrated by
JOAN SANDIN

A Charlotte Zolotow Book

Harper & Row, Publishers

Library of Congress Cataloging-in-Publication Data
Fisher, Aileen Lucia, 1906–
  The house of a mouse : poems / by Aileen Fisher ; illustrated by
Joan Sandin. — 1st ed.
    p.   cm.
  "A Charlotte Zolotow book."
  Summary: A collection of poems about mice, what they eat, where
they live, and how they look.
  ISBN 0-06-021848-7 : $
  ISBN 0-06-021849-5 (lib. bdg.) : $
  1. Mice—Juvenile poetry.   2. Children's poetry, American.
  [1. Mice—Poetry.   2. American poetry.]   I. Sandin, Joan, ill.
    II. Title.
PS3511.I7294H65   1988
811'.54—dc19   87-24947
                                                           CIP
                                                            AC

Other Books by *Aileen Fisher*

Portrait

Such big eyes
for one so small,
such big ears
to hear-it-all,

Such trim feet
in barefoot shoes,
such long whiskers
full of news,

Such soft fur
to dress you up,
posing near
a buttercup...

That's *you*, little Mouse!

House
Guest

There was a Mouse
whose coat was trim,
whose ears were pink,
whose feet were slim....
It was a timid little Mouse
who slipped inside a lady's house.

The lady saw him.
"H-E-L-P!" she cried.
You'd think a *lion*
had barged inside.
You'd think a *bear* had broken in
instead of just a Mousikin.

Timid
as a
Mouse?

Who says a Mouse is timid?
"Timid as a mouse."
I think a Mouse is brave at night
to venture from his house
and hunt for things to nibble
and grass and twigs to chew,
when eyes are on the watch for him
the whole night through....

Eyes of owls and cats and skunks,
to mention just a few,
watching for a little Mouse
the whole night through.

*Careful,
Mouse!*

The great horned owl
and the gray-eared cat
look something alike.
Have you thought of that?
    And they both catch Mice.

With ear tufts up
and with round, sharp eyes,
the great horned owl
is a big-cat size.
    And they both catch Mice.

But the owl's sharp beak
and the cat's flat nose
are very unlike,
as are their toes.
    But they both catch Mice!

Mouseways

Hidden away
under the hay
out of the sun,
Meadow Mice run.

Sharp little teeth
cut roads beneath
gold hay and green,
narrow, unseen.

Quick little feet
know every street,
but where the streets go
we never know.

Deer
Mouse

Who tells the little Deer Mouse
when summer goes away
that she should fix a cozy place,
a comfy place to stay,
and fill her cupboard shelves with seeds
from berries, weeds, and hay?

Who tells the little Deer Mouse
before the year is old
that she should wear a warmer coat
to shield her from the cold?

I'm glad that SOMEONE tells her
and she does as she is told.

Pockets

How do you carry
those mini-sized seeds
you gather from grasses
and autumn-brown weeds
to store in your cupboard
for cold-weather needs,
little Mouse?

I know! You have pockets
without any leaks
for toting home seeds
that will last you for weeks.
And where are your pockets?
Inside of your cheeks,
little Mouse!

First
Snow

When autumn stills
the crickets
and yellow leaves turn brown,
I wonder what
a Mouseling thinks
as snow starts falling down,
and petal
after petal
goes trickling down his nose
and there's
a strange, cold tickle
between his slender toes?

First Snowfall

The little Mouse
in her knothole house,
where her bed is warm and dry...
does she get a shock
when it's snow o'clock
and whiteness fills the sky?

She only knows
about grass that grows,
and weed stalks turned to gold.
She never has heard
a single word
about the snow and cold.

On a sudden night
when the world turns white
and green and gold are through,
the little Mouse
in her knothole house…
does she wonder what to do?

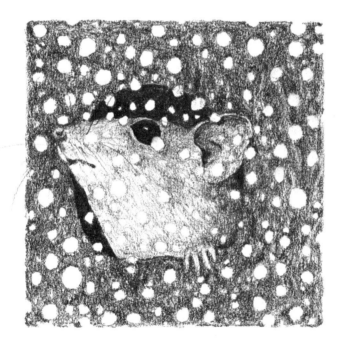

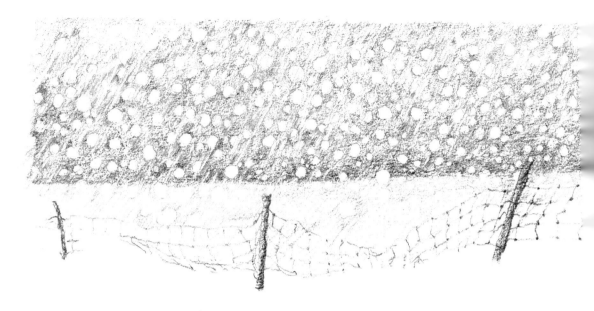

When It's Snowing

Little Mouse, with narrow feet
that you keep so white and neat,
when it's snowing, freezing, blowing,
do you get enough to eat?

You're too little, Mouse, to stray
from your house on such a day.
Weren't you wise to gather scores
of munchy seeds to eat indoors!

*Under
the
Snow*

Do you know, do you know
where little Mice go
when the meadow is white
with billows of snow?

They dive out of sight
and nibble and play
in tunnels of white
all hidden away…
and if they play "snowballs"
I really can't say.

A Cozy
Little
House

Do you know where a Mouse
built a cozy little house
when summer had gone by?

Not in a hole,
like a scratchy little mole,
but under the hazy sky.

A nest like a muff
made of cattail fluff
on a cattail that was dry…

That's where a Mouse
built a cozy little house,
and that's where so would I.

Winter
Nests

I wonder if the bluebirds know
in the southland where they go
that now the weeds wear fluffy caps
and hills have covers on their laps
and all the nests are full of snow
except the one that makes a house
for little Mrs. Whitefoot Mouse?

Christmas Mouse

On the soft white snow
there's a thin white track
where a little Mouse ran
but didn't come back…
for close to some rocks
where the tall weeds lean
the little Mouse changed
to a submarine!

At the foot of a fir
he ducked down under—
does he live in a house
down there, I wonder,
with a wreath on his door
for his friends to see,
and a sprig of spruce
for a Christmas tree?

Snow
Stitches

Who's the one
in winter's house
who likes to stitch and sew?

Around the meadow's
new white blouse
some dainty footprints go.

No, not a hare.
No, not a grouse.
But just a plucky little Mouse…

That's the one
whose footprints show
like stitches in the new white snow.

The
House
of a
Mouse

The tiny world of Meadow Mice
can't be very safe and nice

When nibbly sheep and crunchy cows
make earthquake-trembles as they browse,

And horses plunk a giant hoof
beside (or on) a Mouse's roof.

I'm glad *my* house is stronger far
than Mouses' houses ever are.

A Mouse and Her House

A Mouse has a house
but she doesn't keep it tidy.

She doesn't use a mop
from Friday to Friday.

She doesn't sweep her room
with a broom on Monday
or Tuesday or Wednesday
or right through Sunday.

But a Mouse in a blouse
of velveteen is tidy
when it comes to *herself*
from Friday to Friday:

She washes her hands,
her fingers, her toes,
her ears and her whiskers,
her tail and her nose.

She washes the fur
of her velvety clothes
not only on Friday,
but Thursday and Sunday
and Tuesday and Wednesday
and Saturday and Monday.

Surprise

I wonder…
does Mrs. Meadow Mouse
dust off her jacket
and smooth her blouse
and ask her neighbors
to stop their labors
and hurry to see
her big surprise—

Six little babies
with tight-shut eyes,
curling together
(as Mouselings do),
rosy and dozy
and squeaky new?

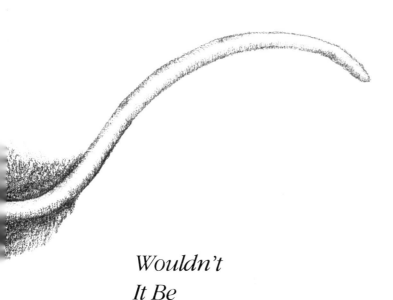

Wouldn't It Be Queer?

"Come and eat your dish of seeds,
Come and drink your dew.
Try these green and tender weeds—
they are good for you.

"Brush away the crumbs you find,
comb your whiskers nice...."
Wouldn't it be queer to mind
parents who were MICE?